Celebrating
FAMILY
TRADITIONS

Celebrating FAMILY TRADITIONS

An Idea and Keepsake Book

BY HELEN BAINE BLAND & MARY SEEHAFER SEARS

Illustrated by Patti Falzarano

A BULFINCH PRESS BOOK / LITTLE, BROWN AND COMPANY
BOSTON • NEW YORK • TORONTO • LONDON

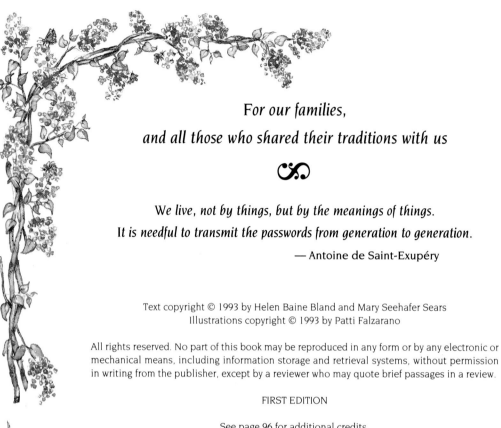

For our families,

and all those who shared their traditions with us

We live, not by things, but by the meanings of things.
It is needful to transmit the passwords from generation to generation.

— Antoine de Saint-Exupéry

FIRST EDITION

See page 96 for additional credits.

Library of Congress Cataloging–in–Publication Data
Bland, Helen Baine.
    Celebrating family traditions: an idea and keepsake book for all kinds of families / Helen Baine Bland and Mary Seehafer Sears ; illustrated by Patti Falzarano.
        p.   cm.
    "A Bulfinch Press book."
    ISBN 0-8212-2004-7
    1. Family festivals — United States.   2. United States — Social life and customs.   I. Sears, Mary Seehafer.   II. Title.
GT2402.U6B53 1993   93-3608
394.2'6—dc20

Designed by Jeanne Abboud

Bulfinch Press is an imprint and trademark of Little, Brown and Company (Inc.)
Published simultaneously in Canada by Little, Brown & Company (Canada) Limited

PRINTED IN SINGAPORE

CONTENTS

INTRODUCTION

Our book began quite by accident several years ago, when each of us decided to write down our family traditions as keepsakes for our children. Instead of simply recording "family roots," our focus was on specific, personal family occasions we wanted to remember and sustain. In hectic times, we felt there was a certain comfort in knowing who puts the star on the Christmas tree every year and who raises the flag during vacations at the lake. And we didn't want to forget the jokes, shenanigans, and events that had brightened so many of our times together.

Little did we know how intriguing our idea would be to others. When we shared our books with friends, they were eager to read how another family celebrated life ("almost as much fun as reading someone's diary," said one), and they would inevitably chime in with their own cherished traditions and rituals. Some recollections were personal and touching; many were downright funny. We soon realized we had the makings of a book on our hands. It seemed as though everyone wanted to share a unique tradition.

Gradually, our pool of contributors expanded. Friends, friends of friends, and acquaintances who have lived all over the world shared their lives with us. The common thread in what we've heard is how important parents, family, and friends are, not only when we're young, but all through our lives.

Americans have always had a penchant for grand traditions like Fourth of July and Thanksgiving, but no less important are the hundreds of small traditions that begin in a simple way. These traditions persist because they strike a chord of comfort within us. They express our personality and give strength and nourishment and a sense of renewal to our days and our family spirit.

For today's far-flung families, traditions assume added importance. They keep us in touch with our roots. And when traditions are firmly in place, they give us another advantage: the freedom to sit back and enjoy our special occasions. If the framework of an event is a long-established tradition, much of the planning is already done. This can be a boon for working families, who still want to celebrate important times in the midst of busy lives.

This is an idea book for those who are searching for ways to establish their own unique celebrations. It's also a keepsake — a place to write down ideas and thoughts, your own traditions in the making, or events from your childhood you'd like to repeat.

It's a book for *all* kinds of families — whether your "family" is relatives, friends, people you work with, your neighbors, or just you and your dog. It is a salute to ideas that blossomed into traditions because they generated love, warmth, laughter, and joy and strengthened the bonds between ourselves and our families or our friends.

We dedicate this book to those unique, quirky, ever-intriguing customs that give us a peg on which to hang our family hat; to those traditions that last and allow us to pass something of ourselves on to the next generation.

THROUGH THE YEAR

୧୨

Traditions for All Seasons

Christmas is the mainstay of my year because tradition is the mainstay of my life. It keeps me whole. It is the centrifugal force that stops the pieces from shooting wildly into the void. The only way I can bear the changes that grind on inexorably around me is to pepper the year with those things that never change. Bath and books for the boys before bedtime. Homemade cakes on their birthdays. The beach in August. Chestnuts roasting on an open fire. Jack Frost nipping at your nose. You name it, I do it.

— Anna Quindlen, *Living Out Loud*

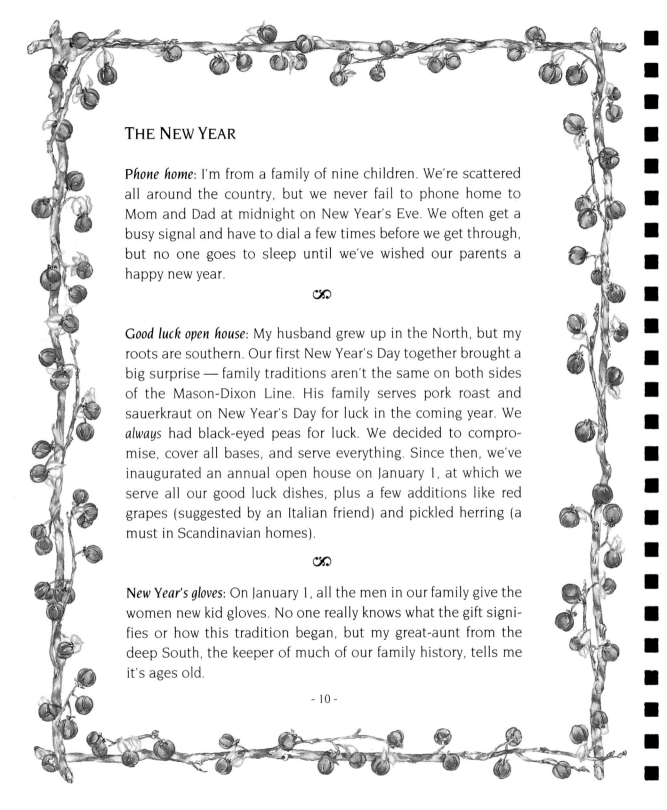

THE NEW YEAR

Phone home: I'm from a family of nine children. We're scattered all around the country, but we never fail to phone home to Mom and Dad at midnight on New Year's Eve. We often get a busy signal and have to dial a few times before we get through, but no one goes to sleep until we've wished our parents a happy new year.

ⅭⅩⅮ

Good luck open house: My husband grew up in the North, but my roots are southern. Our first New Year's Day together brought a big surprise — family traditions aren't the same on both sides of the Mason-Dixon Line. His family serves pork roast and sauerkraut on New Year's Day for luck in the coming year. We *always* had black-eyed peas for luck. We decided to compromise, cover all bases, and serve everything. Since then, we've inaugurated an annual open house on January 1, at which we serve all our good luck dishes, plus a few additions like red grapes (suggested by an Italian friend) and pickled herring (a must in Scandinavian homes).

ⅭⅩⅮ

New Year's gloves: On January 1, all the men in our family give the women new kid gloves. No one really knows what the gift signifies or how this tradition began, but my great-aunt from the deep South, the keeper of much of our family history, tells me it's ages old.

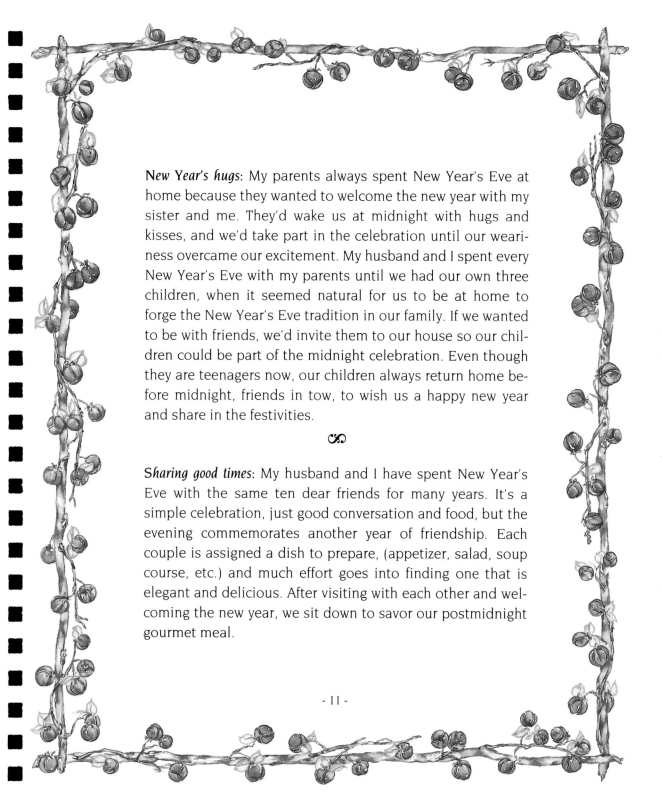

New Year's hugs: My parents always spent New Year's Eve at home because they wanted to welcome the new year with my sister and me. They'd wake us at midnight with hugs and kisses, and we'd take part in the celebration until our weariness overcame our excitement. My husband and I spent every New Year's Eve with my parents until we had our own three children, when it seemed natural for us to be at home to forge the New Year's Eve tradition in our family. If we wanted to be with friends, we'd invite them to our house so our children could be part of the midnight celebration. Even though they are teenagers now, our children always return home before midnight, friends in tow, to wish us a happy new year and share in the festivities.

∽

Sharing good times: My husband and I have spent New Year's Eve with the same ten dear friends for many years. It's a simple celebration, just good conversation and food, but the evening commemorates another year of friendship. Each couple is assigned a dish to prepare, (appetizer, salad, soup course, etc.) and much effort goes into finding one that is elegant and delicious. After visiting with each other and welcoming the new year, we sit down to savor our postmidnight gourmet meal.

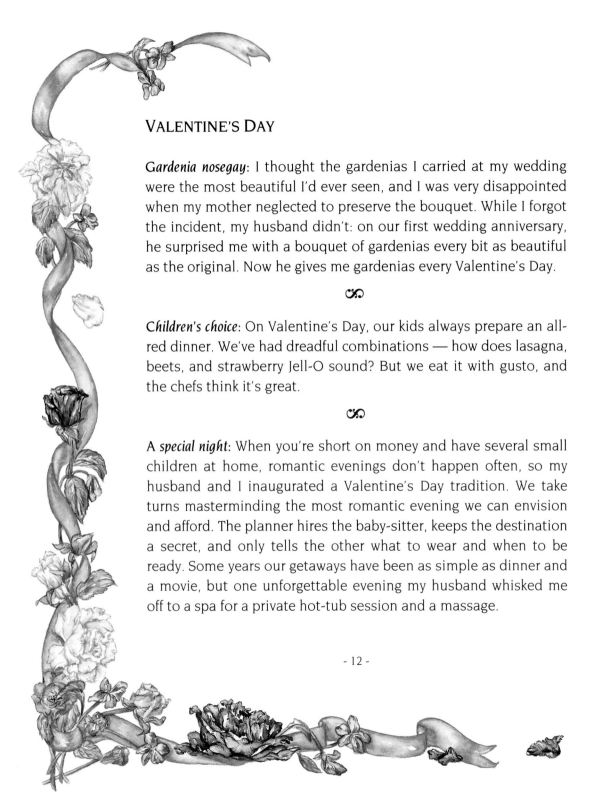

VALENTINE'S DAY

Gardenia nosegay: I thought the gardenias I carried at my wedding were the most beautiful I'd ever seen, and I was very disappointed when my mother neglected to preserve the bouquet. While I forgot the incident, my husband didn't: on our first wedding anniversary, he surprised me with a bouquet of gardenias every bit as beautiful as the original. Now he gives me gardenias every Valentine's Day.

☙

Children's choice: On Valentine's Day, our kids always prepare an all-red dinner. We've had dreadful combinations — how does lasagna, beets, and strawberry Jell-O sound? But we eat it with gusto, and the chefs think it's great.

☙

A *special night*: When you're short on money and have several small children at home, romantic evenings don't happen often, so my husband and I inaugurated a Valentine's Day tradition. We take turns masterminding the most romantic evening we can envision and afford. The planner hires the baby-sitter, keeps the destination a secret, and only tells the other what to wear and when to be ready. Some years our getaways have been as simple as dinner and a movie, but one unforgettable evening my husband whisked me off to a spa for a private hot-tub session and a massage.

Cards, cards, cards: Since I'm a hopeless romantic, my favorite holiday is Valentine's Day. I remember how happy — and important — I felt when I was young, carrying home the box full of cards given to me by classmates. Now that I'm married, my husband and I recapture that feeling by making a big to-do every Valentine's Day. We buy each other about a dozen cards — some humorous, some romantic. A few are mailed to the office, the rest we present in the morning and after work. The last ones are reserved for our pillows.

༼༽

Creative valentines: Our kids make their own valentines, just as my mother taught me to do. We take their drawings to a quick-print place, and request red ink on white paper. These cards are a hit with grandparents and the kids at school. We use the leftovers as thank you notes.

༼༽

Sweet valentines: When my mother celebrates Valentine's Day, she gets the jump on Easter by giving each of us a chocolate egg with our name written on top in white icing. If anyone in the family has a serious romance going, that boyfriend or girlfriend gets an egg, too, and this is considered the official nod of acceptance from Mom.

SPRINGTIME

Bunny tracks: When my children were young, I'd dip my fingers in flour on the night before Easter and plant bunny tracks around the house leading to their Easter baskets. The children always loved following the trail, and I loved seeing their shining faces on the hunt. They're in college now and believe it or not, the kids still drop by on Easter Day to look for the bunny tracks!

Daffodil days: When the American Cancer Society has its Daffodil Days at the end of March, I buy bunches of the golden flowers to brighten my co-workers' desks. I don't tell them why, but I do it as a tribute to my mother, who had cancer.

May baskets: Every May Day, my daughter and I make May baskets for our neighbors. They're simple little baskets — just construction paper cones with stapled-on handles. The fun is in running around our yard and the woods across the street to gather pretty grasses and spring flowers to tuck inside. Then it's off to hang the baskets on front doorknobs as a spring surprise.

Mother's Day in the park: We always invite friends to join us for a Mother's Day picnic brunch in the park featuring Dad as the cook. The menu is classic: sausage, scrambled eggs with peppers and onions cooked in a black skillet on the grill, and plenty of juice and coffee. The kids toast bagels over the fire, and all the moms get to put their feet up.

ᛣᗢ

Spring walk: Our annual spring-cleaning doesn't stop with our house. After we throw away the clutter and get rid of winter cobwebs, we fan out over the neighborhood, carrying large garbage bags. Our goal: to rid the area of the trash that has accumulated under the snow during the winter months. Many of our neighbors come out to help when they see us on patrol.

ᛣᗢ

Window-washing party: My parents' Victorian house has lots of windows. When we were young and it was spring-cleaning time, my mother enlisted the five of us as window washers. We'd spend the day balanced on ladders or hanging out upstairs windows, holding wadded up newspapers and spray bottles of her magic ammonia-and-water mixture. By the time we finished, the windows twinkled like jewels. Now, years later, we still heed Mom's yearly summons to her window-washing party.

SUMMERTIME

Jennie's garden: When my four-year-old granddaughter arrived for a week-long visit in early summer, I was so excited I wanted to make her visit something she'd remember all year long. So we planted a garden just for her. We worked the soil and pulled out rocks, but it wasn't until we reached the nursery that she became a true gardener. "Nana, look at the beautiful flowers!" She wanted one of everything. It was a lesson in bargaining and compromising, but we finally emerged with an armful of plants that we set in the ground. The final touch was a little sign marking it as "Jennie's Garden." I sent pictures to her all summer so she could see how her flowers were growing. An avid gardener now, she visits every year to tend her little patch of ground.

Big bang: We've lived around the world, but no matter where we find ourselves on the Fourth of July, we celebrate in all-American style. We listen to Copland's "Fanfare for the Common Man," then we shoot off a two-foot cannon (an anniversary gift from my Dad), which gives us a noise and a flash — our own little "shot heard 'round the world."

Sweet vacation: My husband and I watch our young daughter's sugar intake — except on our yearly vacation, when she's allowed to choose any breakfast cereal she wants.

Trip tins: My sister and I spent many vacations with my aunt, who was famous for her sugar cookies. At the end of our visit, she always presented each of us with our own personal tin of cookies. We were allowed to eat these as we pleased during the long car trip home. (We loved not having to share.) There were also little wrapped surprises to open along the way. I have such pleasant memories of those little treat boxes that I plan to make some for my twins as soon as they're old enough to enjoy them.

⌒⌒

Wishing boats: At our summer cottage by the lake, we make paper boats and pick a clear, starry night to launch them. We light a birthday candle inside each one and make a wish before putting them out to sea. Then we sit on the dock and watch until our little armada is out of sight.

⌒⌒

Goodbye, summer: It's sad to see summer just fizzle to an end, so we always have a "Goodbye Summer Party" the week before school starts. I pile the kids in the car and drive to the beach, where we spend a carefree day in the sun with kites, balloons, body boards, sand-castle contests, and an old-fashioned clambake at sunset. By the time we reach home we know we've grandly said farewell to our favorite season of the year.

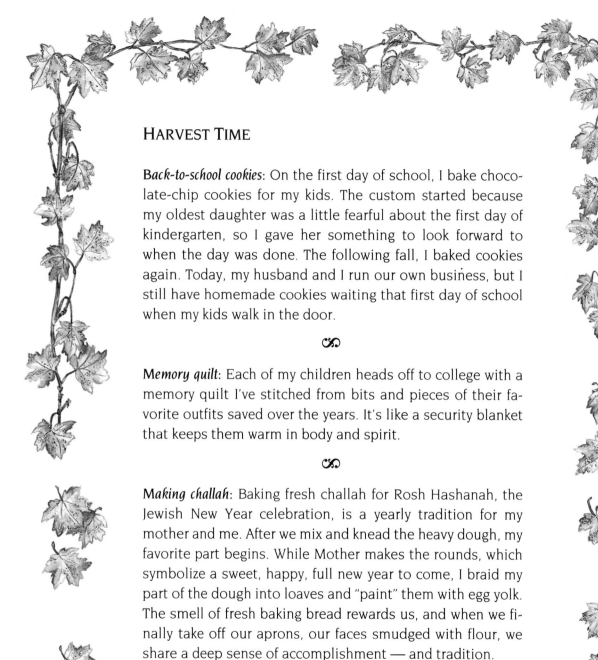

HARVEST TIME

Back-to-school cookies: On the first day of school, I bake chocolate-chip cookies for my kids. The custom started because my oldest daughter was a little fearful about the first day of kindergarten, so I gave her something to look forward to when the day was done. The following fall, I baked cookies again. Today, my husband and I run our own business, but I still have homemade cookies waiting that first day of school when my kids walk in the door.

ॐ

Memory quilt: Each of my children heads off to college with a memory quilt I've stitched from bits and pieces of their favorite outfits saved over the years. It's like a security blanket that keeps them warm in body and spirit.

ॐ

Making challah: Baking fresh challah for Rosh Hashanah, the Jewish New Year celebration, is a yearly tradition for my mother and me. After we mix and knead the heavy dough, my favorite part begins. While Mother makes the rounds, which symbolize a sweet, happy, full new year to come, I braid my part of the dough into loaves and "paint" them with egg yolk. The smell of fresh baking bread rewards us, and when we finally take off our aprons, our faces smudged with flour, we share a deep sense of accomplishment — and tradition.

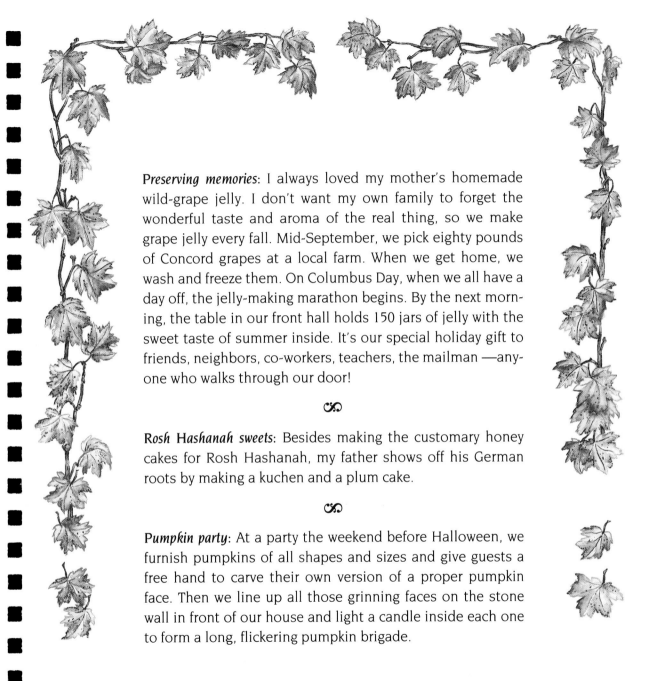

Preserving memories: I always loved my mother's homemade wild-grape jelly. I don't want my own family to forget the wonderful taste and aroma of the real thing, so we make grape jelly every fall. Mid-September, we pick eighty pounds of Concord grapes at a local farm. When we get home, we wash and freeze them. On Columbus Day, when we all have a day off, the jelly-making marathon begins. By the next morning, the table in our front hall holds 150 jars of jelly with the sweet taste of summer inside. It's our special holiday gift to friends, neighbors, co-workers, teachers, the mailman —anyone who walks through our door!

ॐ

Rosh Hashanah sweets: Besides making the customary honey cakes for Rosh Hashanah, my father shows off his German roots by making a kuchen and a plum cake.

ॐ

Pumpkin party: At a party the weekend before Halloween, we furnish pumpkins of all shapes and sizes and give guests a free hand to carve their own version of a proper pumpkin face. Then we line up all those grinning faces on the stone wall in front of our house and light a candle inside each one to form a long, flickering pumpkin brigade.

Job jar: No one likes to get stuck with all the work on Thanksgiving, so we divide it up. Small slips of paper listing all the jobs to be done are dropped into a big jar or empty spaghetti pot. Each person grabs a paper and does whatever job is written there, such as make a flower arrangement, mash potatoes, or serve dessert. A few simple tasks are put in a little pot for the younger set, and they do chores like folding napkins, making placecards, and laying out the silverware.

ᥰ

Thanksgiving breakfast: My mother and I have followed the same tradition every Thanksgiving for as long as I can remember. We get up early and put our breakfasts on a tray. Then, still dressed in pajamas and bathrobes, we watch the annual Thanksgiving parade on television. The color and pageantry are great, but best of all is having this special mother-daughter morning together.

ᥰ

Rite of passage: At the end of our Thanksgiving dinner, a toast is offered by every person seated at the "adults' table." Sometimes the toasts are a tribute to a family member, sometimes an account of shared history. This tradition serves as a rite of passage for our youngsters: when they feel confident enough to propose a toast, they leave the children's table and eat with the grown-ups. We've been entertained — and amused — by these toasts through the years. My son even wrote about this tradition on his college application when asked to recount something that means a lot to him.

A *Friday Thanksgiving*: Now that my brothers and sisters and I are married and have spouses' relatives to contend with as well as our own, my mother always has Thanksgiving dinner at her house the day after the holiday. Almost everyone has the day off. This tradition allows us to satisfy *all* our families.

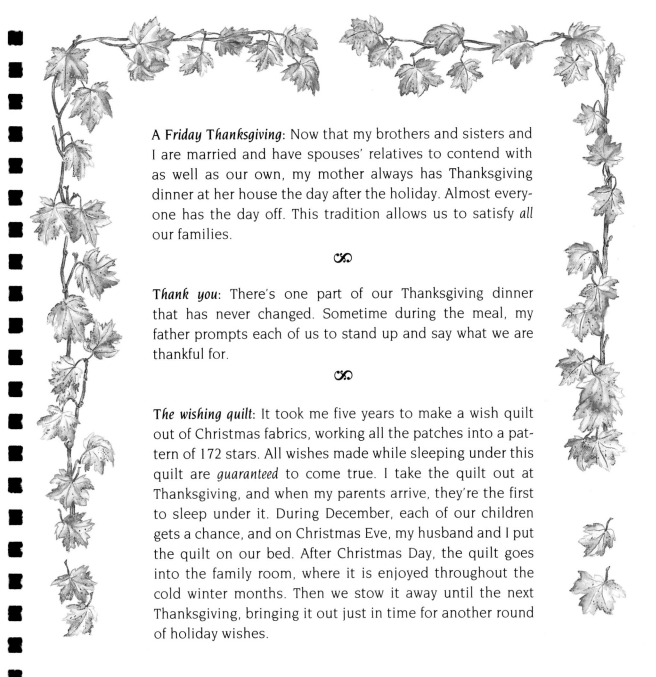

Thank you: There's one part of our Thanksgiving dinner that has never changed. Sometime during the meal, my father prompts each of us to stand up and say what we are thankful for.

The wishing quilt: It took me five years to make a wish quilt out of Christmas fabrics, working all the patches into a pattern of 172 stars. All wishes made while sleeping under this quilt are *guaranteed* to come true. I take the quilt out at Thanksgiving, and when my parents arrive, they're the first to sleep under it. During December, each of our children gets a chance, and on Christmas Eve, my husband and I put the quilt on our bed. After Christmas Day, the quilt goes into the family room, where it is enjoyed throughout the cold winter months. Then we stow it away until the next Thanksgiving, bringing it out just in time for another round of holiday wishes.

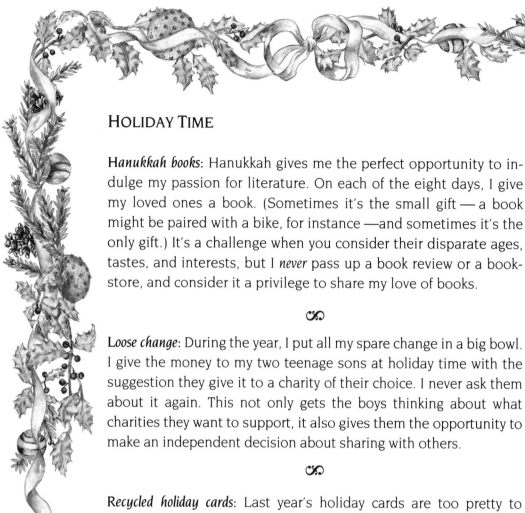

HOLIDAY TIME

Hanukkah books: Hanukkah gives me the perfect opportunity to indulge my passion for literature. On each of the eight days, I give my loved ones a book. (Sometimes it's the small gift — a book might be paired with a bike, for instance —and sometimes it's the only gift.) It's a challenge when you consider their disparate ages, tastes, and interests, but I *never* pass up a book review or a bookstore, and consider it a privilege to share my love of books.

&

Loose change: During the year, I put all my spare change in a big bowl. I give the money to my two teenage sons at holiday time with the suggestion they give it to a charity of their choice. I never ask them about it again. This not only gets the boys thinking about what charities they want to support, it also gives them the opportunity to make an independent decision about sharing with others.

&

Recycled holiday cards: Last year's holiday cards are too pretty to waste, so I recycle them as gift tags for this year's presents, using simple wrapping papers (solids, stripes, and polka dots) to show them off. Rereading those old cards is like getting a whole mailbox full of letters at once.

&

Decorating party: We bake Christmas cookies throughout December but my mother never lets us eat them until tree-decorating night, which is a food fest at our house. We start with hot soup and finger foods and eat and decorate until the tree is full. Then it's *finally* cookie time.

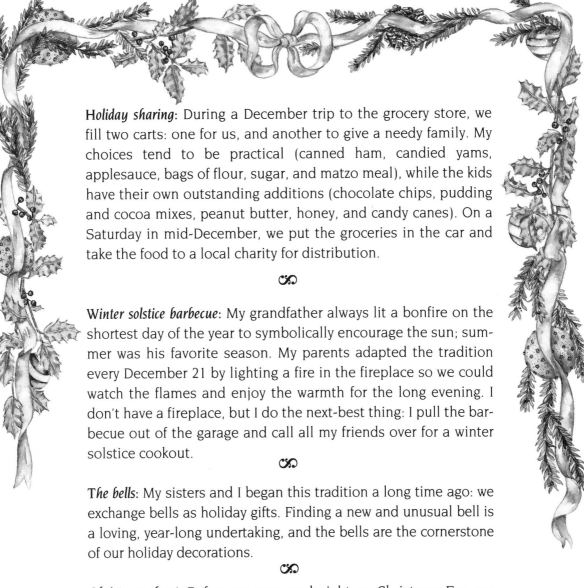

Holiday sharing: During a December trip to the grocery store, we fill two carts: one for us, and another to give a needy family. My choices tend to be practical (canned ham, candied yams, applesauce, bags of flour, sugar, and matzo meal), while the kids have their own outstanding additions (chocolate chips, pudding and cocoa mixes, peanut butter, honey, and candy canes). On a Saturday in mid-December, we put the groceries in the car and take the food to a local charity for distribution.

Winter solstice barbecue: My grandfather always lit a bonfire on the shortest day of the year to symbolically encourage the sun; summer was his favorite season. My parents adapted the tradition every December 21 by lighting a fire in the fireplace so we could watch the flames and enjoy the warmth for the long evening. I don't have a fireplace, but I do the next-best thing: I pull the barbecue out of the garage and call all my friends over for a winter solstice cookout.

The bells: My sisters and I began this tradition a long time ago: we exchange bells as holiday gifts. Finding a new and unusual bell is a loving, year-long undertaking, and the bells are the cornerstone of our holiday decorations.

Christmas chant: Before we say good-night on Christmas Eve, we chant an old English carol that always leaves us laughing: "We wish you a merry Christmas/And a happy new year/A pocket full of money/And a cellar full of beer/And a great fat pig to last you all the year."

Vacation ornaments: Every time our family takes a vacation, we bring back a Christmas ornament that typifies the area we've visited. My personal favorites are a lobster from Maine, a Mickey Mouse bought at Disney World, and a replica of the Golden Gate Bridge from San Francisco. When we decorate our tree, these ornaments initiate a round of vacation memories. And holiday visitors are always intrigued by our one-of-a-kind Christmas tree.

❧

Citizenship trees: Each holiday season I show appreciation for my adopted country, the United States, in a way that's enjoyed by all the members of our small community. My wife and I have planted our hillside with Norway pine and blue spruce trees, which remind me of my native Switzerland. We decorate the trees for Christmas, each year extending the decorations to one additional tree to signify another year of my citizenship. By the time we finish this year there will be forty-four trees decorated with five thousand small white lights. Our house sits on a hill overlooking a large pond, and the reflection of the lighted trees in the water magnifies their beauty. Our neighbors have even jokingly offered to pay our electric bill because they love the sight!

❧

Gingerbread-house party: Making a gingerbread house is quite an undertaking, but doing it as a group makes it fun. Every year my extended family gets together to make one giant gingerbread house, which stays at the home of the hostess. You can always tell the house has had many "carpenters," but that's what makes it charming. Each person also makes a small house to take home.

Julbukk: One of the most thoughtful gifts we received at our wedding was a little straw horse, called a *julbukk*. In my Norwegian family, it's a custom to place the *julbukk* under the Christmas tree to ensure good fortune for the year ahead, and my friends knew I'd want one to carry on this tradition in my new household.

☙

Shopping date: Many years ago I dragged my husband along on a holiday shopping trip. I had young children, a long list, and was desperate for help. After a marathon shopping day, we stopped at a small restaurant for a quiet dinner — alone. We haven't missed a holiday shopping date since. After our own three kids graduated from the toy department, we were still there, enchanted as we watched other people's children discover the wonders of the holiday season. Since then, we've come full circle. We're shopping for four grandchildren now.

☙

Candlelight Christmas Eve: I have a large collection of candlesticks from garage sales and flea markets. I fill them with red candles and group them throughout the house at holiday time. On Christmas Eve, we light all the candles, turn off the lights except those on the tree, and enjoy the spectacle. Dinner is by candlelight, and we gather in front of the living room fireplace afterward for coffee and dessert. My husband plays his guitar and we sing our favorite carols. Then right before bed, we read *The Night Before Christmas* aloud.

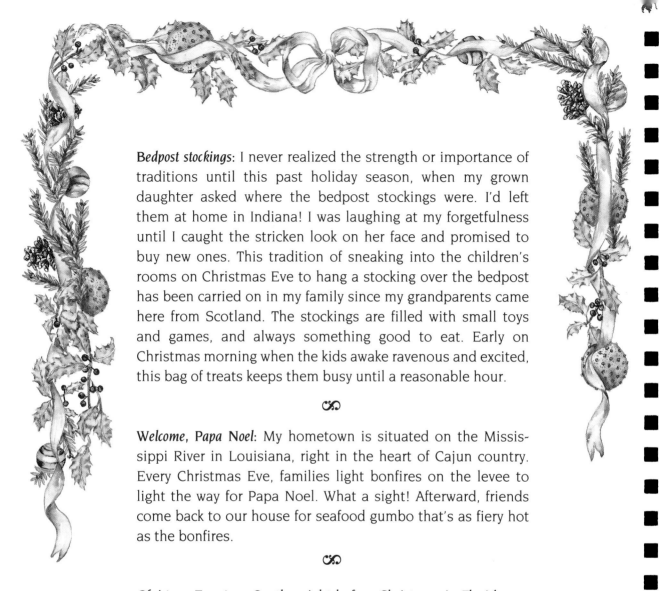

Bedpost stockings: I never realized the strength or importance of traditions until this past holiday season, when my grown daughter asked where the bedpost stockings were. I'd left them at home in Indiana! I was laughing at my forgetfulness until I caught the stricken look on her face and promised to buy new ones. This tradition of sneaking into the children's rooms on Christmas Eve to hang a stocking over the bedpost has been carried on in my family since my grandparents came here from Scotland. The stockings are filled with small toys and games, and always something good to eat. Early on Christmas morning when the kids awake ravenous and excited, this bag of treats keeps them busy until a reasonable hour.

చౌ

Welcome, Papa Noel: My hometown is situated on the Mississippi River in Louisiana, right in the heart of Cajun country. Every Christmas Eve, families light bonfires on the levee to light the way for Papa Noel. What a sight! Afterward, friends come back to our house for seafood gumbo that's as fiery hot as the bonfires.

చౌ

Christmas Eve story: On the night before Christmas in Florida, we use literature to transport ourselves to snowy surroundings. Each of us reads a passage from Dorothy Sayers's "Necklace of Pearls," a short mystery story set on a wintry Christmas Eve in England.

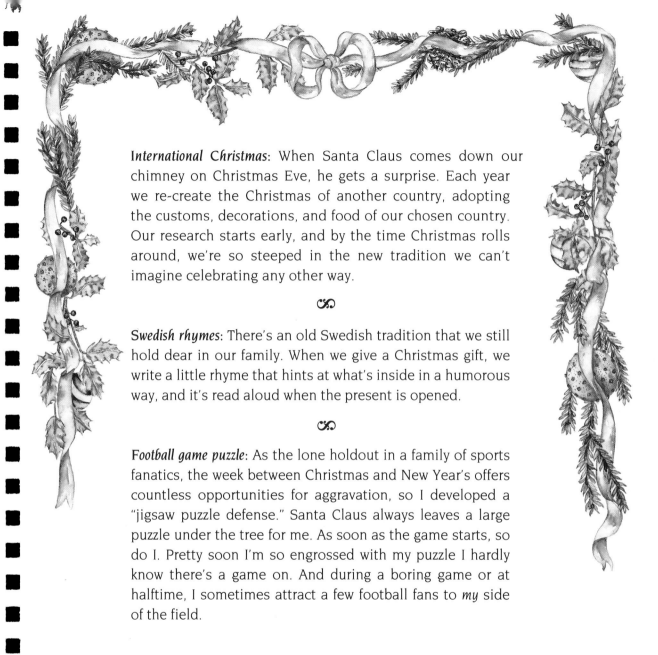

International Christmas: When Santa Claus comes down our chimney on Christmas Eve, he gets a surprise. Each year we re-create the Christmas of another country, adopting the customs, decorations, and food of our chosen country. Our research starts early, and by the time Christmas rolls around, we're so steeped in the new tradition we can't imagine celebrating any other way.

ℭℬ

Swedish rhymes: There's an old Swedish tradition that we still hold dear in our family. When we give a Christmas gift, we write a little rhyme that hints at what's inside in a humorous way, and it's read aloud when the present is opened.

ℭℬ

Football game puzzle: As the lone holdout in a family of sports fanatics, the week between Christmas and New Year's offers countless opportunities for aggravation, so I developed a "jigsaw puzzle defense." Santa Claus always leaves a large puzzle under the tree for me. As soon as the game starts, so do I. Pretty soon I'm so engrossed with my puzzle I hardly know there's a game on. And during a boring game or at halftime, I sometimes attract a few football fans to *my* side of the field.

FAMILY GATHERINGS

Traditions for the History Book

I n these days of scattered families, the ties that bind are like lines on a map, radiating out in all directions. A family or a group of friends whose connections are tight can be a powerful force against the hectic pace of modern life, an antidote to our sense of separation. And who else can we count on to laugh at our jokes? Gatherings large and small provide us with opportunities to retell mutual history and share new experiences, to revel in each other's strengths and foibles, and to celebrate our sameness *and* our diversity.

The summer games: At our annual summer reunions, the Crazy Olympics for the kids is the favorite activity. The emphasis is on fun instead of competition. The action begins with a grand parade of athletes, the youngest child proudly bearing the Olympic torch, fashioned out of rolled-up newspaper wrapped in aluminum foil. The events are easy and suitably silly, including the backwards race, the under-the-leg-Frisbee-toss, and the skipping event. At the awards ceremony in the evening *everyone* gets a medal.

ॐ

Once-a-month dinner: Three of my college friends have become like family to me. After graduation we ended up working in the same city. To keep in touch, we casually started getting together for dinner once a month, with each person taking a turn as host. That was fourteen years ago, and in that time we've been through many joys and sorrows, including marriage, divorce, countless birthdays, several births, and a thousand recipes. Some nights our dinner and conversation are outstanding; sometimes they're not. But someone always rallies the others to continue month after month. Even after one of us moved to the suburbs, the tradition couldn't be squelched. The reward at the end of an hour-long train ride is a home-cooked meal with dearest friends.

Future heirloom: My cousin made a beautiful christening gown for my first daughter, and I hand-embroidered it with flowers. All of my children have been christened in this gown. Before the ceremony, I embroider the slip of the gown with the child's first and middle name, using pink or blue thread. So far, the gown bears four names, and I hope to pass it down for my children's children.

ꙮ

Puppet show: Whenever our extended family gathers, the children bring their favorite puppets to dinner and entertain us with a show afterward. A café curtain strung across the doorway is their stage, and their efforts are rewarded with thunderous applause from a captive audience.

ꙮ

Reunion auction: One of my aunts cleaned out her attic several years ago and decided to auction the treasures she'd accumulated over a lifetime at a family reunion. The auction was such a success we have one at every reunion now, with each family member contributing an item or two. The most sought-after collectibles are old quilts, picture frames, family pictures, and old books. The proceeds help defray the cost of our next reunion.

Acting out: Our family has a long and proud history, and we think it's important to pass it on to our youngsters. When we get together for reunions, we stage skits depicting family stories, with the kids starring in the lead roles, and we play the tape-recorded remembrances of older family members. One year my cousin composed a song entitled "The Midwife of Woodward County," recalling my grandmother's life and her unusual occupation, and it quickly became a reunion favorite.

Guest chefs: It's a mob scene at our house when our children, their spouses, and our grandchildren gather for their yearly visit. Instead of spending all my time cooking and cleaning up, I ask each couple to take over the dinner chores for one night so I can relax and enjoy the fun. When my grandchildren get a little older, I'll suggest they join the tradition by fixing lunch for the group. Peanut butter, anyone?

Good fairies: When we go on vacation, we pull names from a hat and play good fairy, giving secret gifts or doing favors without being seen. On the last day, each person tries to guess the identity of his or her fairy. To make the game harder, we give atypical gifts and do favors we might not normally do. One year my brother made brownies for my mother, which put her off the scent because he's known as a poor cook. When I got pantyhose, I never imagined my father walking into a drugstore and buying such a thing!

WHEN GUESTS ARRIVE

❧

Traditions with a Welcome

Knowing that guests will soon arrive sends us into a flurry of activity. Whether we welcome them with the sight of lights along a winding path, a pot of geraniums on a picnic table, or by the smell of smoke from a winter fire or a freshly lit barbecue grill, what we want to convey is, "We're glad you're here. We like your company." Another way to welcome guests is to share traditions with them. It's a way of saying, "Please come in and be part of our family."

- 49 -

Written in stone: My children are avid collectors of the smooth, flat rocks from the beach near our summer place. When we're entertaining, the children print the name of each guest on a rock with a marking pen, and the rocks serve as charming placecards at the table. As the season passes, the rocks pile up with countless others in a bowl on the sideboard, and at the end of the summer we arrange them outdoors under the trees. When we come upon these rocks in other years, each name brings back a memory.

CﾟЭ

Hidden frescoes: Stripping wallpaper is a tedious task at best, so we devised a plan to ensure some enthusiasm for the next go-round. When all the old paper is off, we gather friends for an evening and assign each a small patch of wall to decorate in whatever manner they choose. After the decorations are finished, we give ourselves a little time to enjoy our "cave drawings," poems, and random scrawls before we hang the new wallpaper. Then when it's time to redecorate — years later — the wallpaper comes off in a flash because we can't wait to see those old messages underneath.

John Hancock tablecloth: In 1976, my mother made me a bright red holiday tablecloth. Everyone who eats with us between Thanksgiving and New Year's is asked to write their name and the year on it, and later I embroider each signature and date with white embroidery floss. The cloth is our own version of a guest book. So far, we have about 150 names — and there's plenty of room for more.

ॐ

On the rocks: We have an enormous rock in our yard that was a gift from the Ice Age. It's a beauty! When overnight guests visit, we always take their picture on the "big rock." My husband and I treasure these pictures. You can't imagine how different each one is. How many ways can people sit on a rock? But these aren't just couples or families or singles, they're personalities, and their diversity is reflected in these pictures. We get two enlargements: one for them, the other to frame and hang in our hall.

ॐ

Sing for your supper: My sister is famous for her "Sing for Your Supper" parties. She invites about twenty friends, and after hors d'oeuvres each person must perform before my sister serves her four-star red beans and rice. I can't sing a note, but anyone can memorize a poem, as my sister said before her first party, so that's my customary presentation. Others yodel, do magic tricks, tell jokes, sing gospel songs, play the banjo . . . By the time we finally eat, we're marveling at each other's hidden talents.

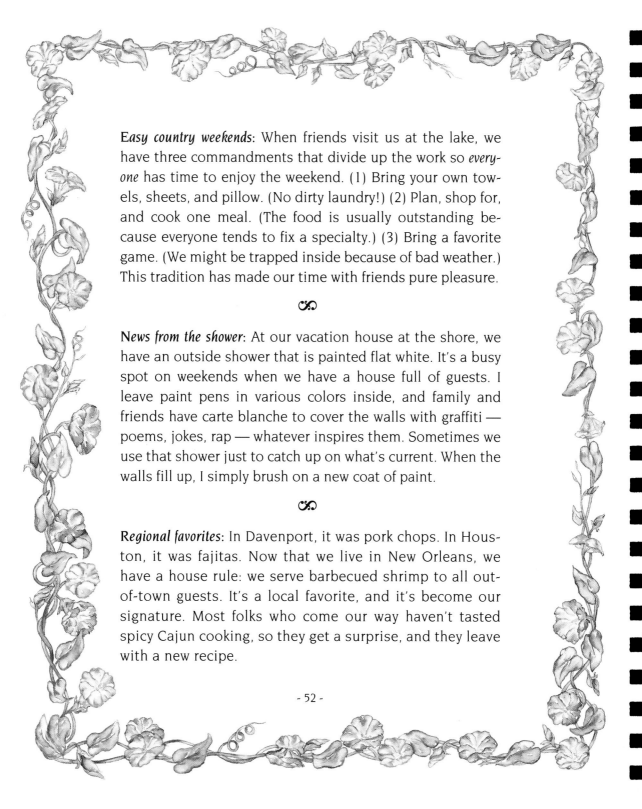

Easy country weekends: When friends visit us at the lake, we have three commandments that divide up the work so *everyone* has time to enjoy the weekend. (1) Bring your own towels, sheets, and pillow. (No dirty laundry!) (2) Plan, shop for, and cook one meal. (The food is usually outstanding because everyone tends to fix a specialty.) (3) Bring a favorite game. (We might be trapped inside because of bad weather.) This tradition has made our time with friends pure pleasure.

છ

News from the shower: At our vacation house at the shore, we have an outside shower that is painted flat white. It's a busy spot on weekends when we have a house full of guests. I leave paint pens in various colors inside, and family and friends have carte blanche to cover the walls with graffiti — poems, jokes, rap — whatever inspires them. Sometimes we use that shower just to catch up on what's current. When the walls fill up, I simply brush on a new coat of paint.

છ

Regional favorites: In Davenport, it was pork chops. In Houston, it was fajitas. Now that we live in New Orleans, we have a house rule: we serve barbecued shrimp to all out-of-town guests. It's a local favorite, and it's become our signature. Most folks who come our way haven't tasted spicy Cajun cooking, so they get a surprise, and they leave with a new recipe.

BIRTHDAY CELEBRATIONS

Traditions with Style

Your birthday: A day to have your cake and eat it, too! By its nature, a birthday is the most personal of occasions — a day that's yours alone. There are as many ways of celebrating birthdays as there are celebrants, and the ways change as we do. So pull out all the stops, put your imagination in gear, light a million candles, go for broke, and make your birthday a day to remember.

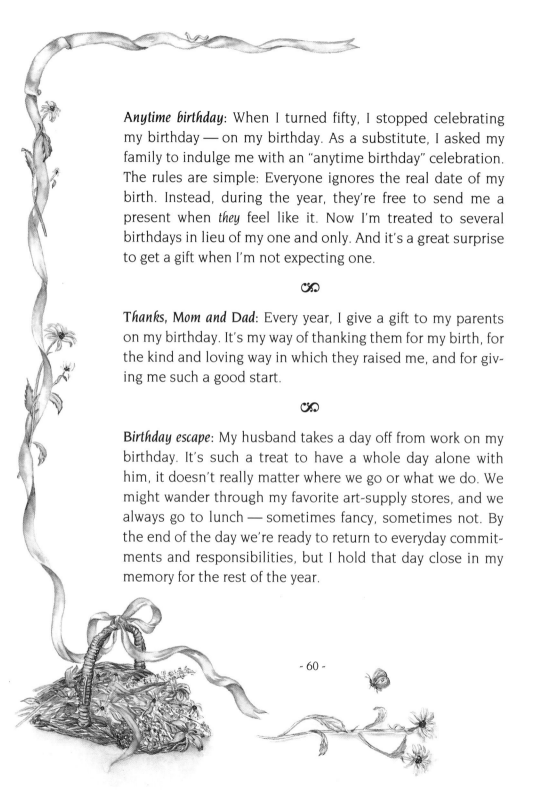

Anytime birthday: When I turned fifty, I stopped celebrating my birthday — on my birthday. As a substitute, I asked my family to indulge me with an "anytime birthday" celebration. The rules are simple: Everyone ignores the real date of my birth. Instead, during the year, they're free to send me a present when *they* feel like it. Now I'm treated to several birthdays in lieu of my one and only. And it's a great surprise to get a gift when I'm not expecting one.

☙

Thanks, Mom and Dad: Every year, I give a gift to my parents on my birthday. It's my way of thanking them for my birth, for the kind and loving way in which they raised me, and for giving me such a good start.

☙

Birthday escape: My husband takes a day off from work on my birthday. It's such a treat to have a whole day alone with him, it doesn't really matter where we go or what we do. We might wander through my favorite art-supply stores, and we always go to lunch — sometimes fancy, sometimes not. By the end of the day we're ready to return to everyday commitments and responsibilities, but I hold that day close in my memory for the rest of the year.

First birthday balloons: One-year-olds and balloons just go together. That's why I send my grandchildren a big bunch of balloons on that important first birthday. Regrettably, I can't always be there, but my kids tell me the colorful balloons bring almost as many smiles as Grandma does.

ᝋ

Happy birthday, house: We think it's good luck to celebrate the day the final papers on our house were signed, so every year we stage a gala dinner. We break out the champagne and set the table with our best china and linen. We're sure our house has a spirit, because the few times we've forgotten, things have happened — plumbing gone berserk, major roof leaks. So we don't forget anymore. During dinner, we toast the house and all the improvements we've made during the year. Then we plan future projects to make our house a more perfect home.

ᝋ

Birthday plate: Someone gave our family a china plate with "Happy Birthday" written on it. If it's your birthday, you eat all three meals off this plate. It makes every bite taste special.

ᝋ

Birthday choice: We take our kids out for lunch on each of their birthdays, and the birthday child gets to choose the restaurant.

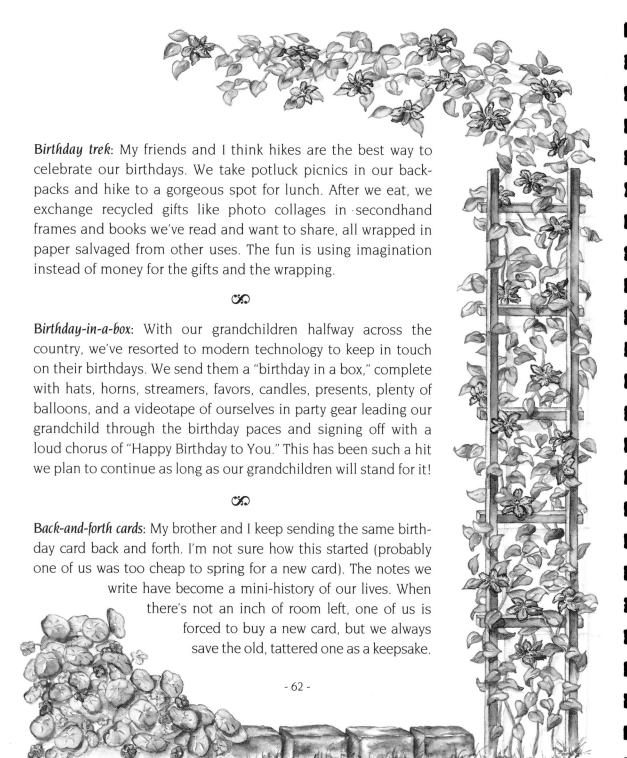

Birthday trek: My friends and I think hikes are the best way to celebrate our birthdays. We take potluck picnics in our backpacks and hike to a gorgeous spot for lunch. After we eat, we exchange recycled gifts like photo collages in secondhand frames and books we've read and want to share, all wrapped in paper salvaged from other uses. The fun is using imagination instead of money for the gifts and the wrapping.

જી

Birthday-in-a-box: With our grandchildren halfway across the country, we've resorted to modern technology to keep in touch on their birthdays. We send them a "birthday in a box," complete with hats, horns, streamers, favors, candles, presents, plenty of balloons, and a videotape of ourselves in party gear leading our grandchild through the birthday paces and signing off with a loud chorus of "Happy Birthday to You." This has been such a hit we plan to continue as long as our grandchildren will stand for it!

જી

Back-and-forth cards: My brother and I keep sending the same birthday card back and forth. I'm not sure how this started (probably one of us was too cheap to spring for a new card). The notes we write have become a mini-history of our lives. When there's not an inch of room left, one of us is forced to buy a new card, but we always save the old, tattered one as a keepsake.

Balloon tree: Each time one of our children has a birthday, my husband and I decorate a tree in our front yard with multicolored balloons to express our joy to them and to all who pass by.

ↅ

Children's gifts from the heart: My husband and I don't *buy* birthday gifts and cards so our young son and daughter are learning that giving something of themselves is the best gift of all. For my husband's birthday, I taught them "He's Got the Whole World in His Hands," which they performed for a happy audience of one. My father was visiting us on his birthday one year, and the kids knew of his passion for strawberries. On their own, they went next door and got permission to pick a big bucket of strawberries from our neighbor's yard, which they proudly presented to their grandpa for his special day. He said it was the sweetest gift he'd ever received.

ↅ

Gifts with imagination: I share an hour or two of weeding time with a birthday friend. . . . I write a "memory story" that recalls fun we've had together. . . . My husband composes birthday poems for our children, recounting highlights of the year. . . . For friends' birthdays, I write a fanciful horoscope for the upcoming year, or make a personalized crossword puzzle.

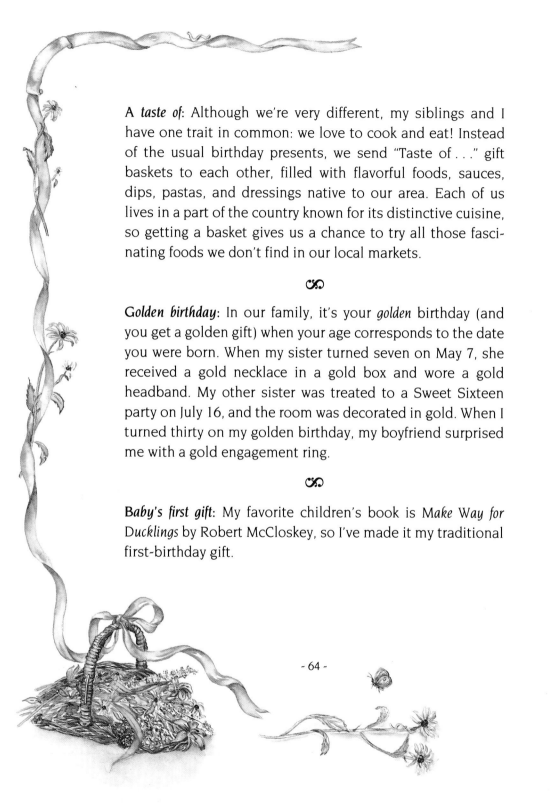

A *taste of*: Although we're very different, my siblings and I have one trait in common: we love to cook and eat! Instead of the usual birthday presents, we send "Taste of . . ." gift baskets to each other, filled with flavorful foods, sauces, dips, pastas, and dressings native to our area. Each of us lives in a part of the country known for its distinctive cuisine, so getting a basket gives us a chance to try all those fascinating foods we don't find in our local markets.

∽

Golden birthday: In our family, it's your *golden* birthday (and you get a golden gift) when your age corresponds to the date you were born. When my sister turned seven on May 7, she received a gold necklace in a gold box and wore a gold headband. My other sister was treated to a Sweet Sixteen party on July 16, and the room was decorated in gold. When I turned thirty on my golden birthday, my boyfriend surprised me with a gold engagement ring.

∽

Baby's first gift: My favorite children's book is *Make Way for Ducklings* by Robert McCloskey, so I've made it my traditional first-birthday gift.

GIFTS FOR THE EARTH

❧

Traditions that Reach Out

Perhaps the most impressive traditions are those that reach beyond friends and family. In gestures large and small, families are taking the long view, casting a wider net to ensure the survival and health of future generations. These traditions seem especially timely in light of our need to make a commitment to the preservation of our planet. They have kindly consequences that will resonate into the next century.

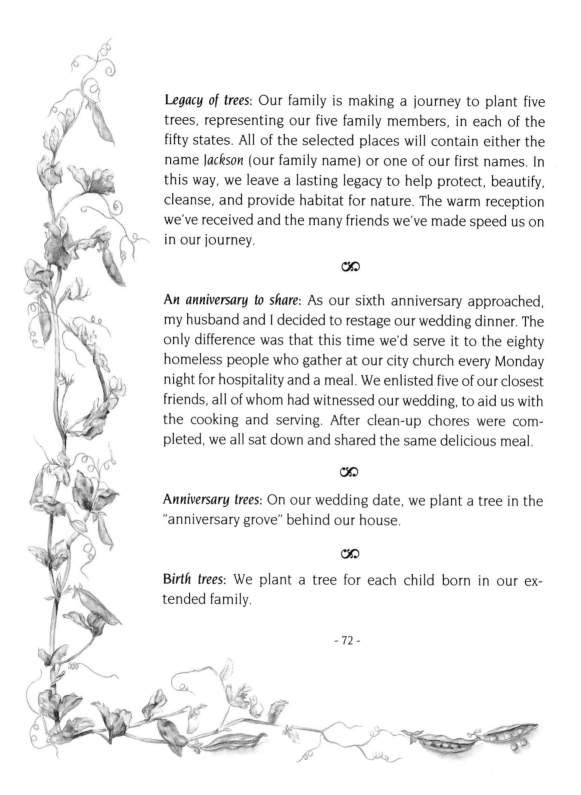

Legacy of trees: Our family is making a journey to plant five trees, representing our five family members, in each of the fifty states. All of the selected places will contain either the name Jackson (our family name) or one of our first names. In this way, we leave a lasting legacy to help protect, beautify, cleanse, and provide habitat for nature. The warm reception we've received and the many friends we've made speed us on in our journey.

CXO

An anniversary to share: As our sixth anniversary approached, my husband and I decided to restage our wedding dinner. The only difference was that this time we'd serve it to the eighty homeless people who gather at our city church every Monday night for hospitality and a meal. We enlisted five of our closest friends, all of whom had witnessed our wedding, to aid us with the cooking and serving. After clean-up chores were completed, we all sat down and shared the same delicious meal.

CXO

Anniversary trees: On our wedding date, we plant a tree in the "anniversary grove" behind our house.

CXO

Birth trees: We plant a tree for each child born in our extended family.

Transfer trees: My husband is always getting transferred. It's hard to move, so while we're pulling up roots, we take time to put some down as well. We plant a tree to leave a little of ourselves behind.

For the birds: We buy a live Christmas tree so we can enjoy it forever. We decorate it with cranberries and popcorn and then plant it outside after the holidays. It's a feast for the birds, and a nesting spot as well.

Adopt-a-whale: Three years ago, I found a gift that's easy on my budget and overwhelmingly popular with recipients. On their behalf, I adopt a humpback whale from the Whale Adoption Project in North Falmouth, Massachusetts, or an orca from the Whale Museum in Friday Harbor, Washington. The recipients receive a picture and description of their whale, a formal adoption certificate, and a newsletter subscription. Now when I give a gift, I'm supporting one of my favorite causes at the same time.

Natural hostess gift: To keep my consumerism at a minimum, my traditional hostess gift is a beautiful basket of fresh produce from my garden or the market.

Friendly fishing: We're a fishing family who believe in the credo "catch and release." To encourage our children to release their catch as quickly and gently as possible, we've taught them to start counting just as they get the fish out of the water and try to release by the time they get to thirty.

Starlight: When there's a death in a close friend's family, we contact the International Star Registry of Ingleside, Illinois, and have a star named in honor of the deceased. We feel this long-lasting memorial conveys the cosmic element of loss. The family receives a map of the universe with names of constellations and galaxies, as well as the coordinates for their star, and a parchment certificate on which the chosen name for the star is printed. We've also used this as a twenty-fifth or fiftieth wedding anniversary gift, and as a special birthday present.

Shoring up the shoreline: My parents' beachfront cottage sits on a point of land that was slowly shrinking because of erosion. Twenty years ago, my father began planting sea grass to protect the property against the ravages of nature. He wanted his grandchildren to enjoy the same carefree summers that we had known. His small yearly efforts have paid off. We join him in the planting each time we visit, preserving the point for generations to come.

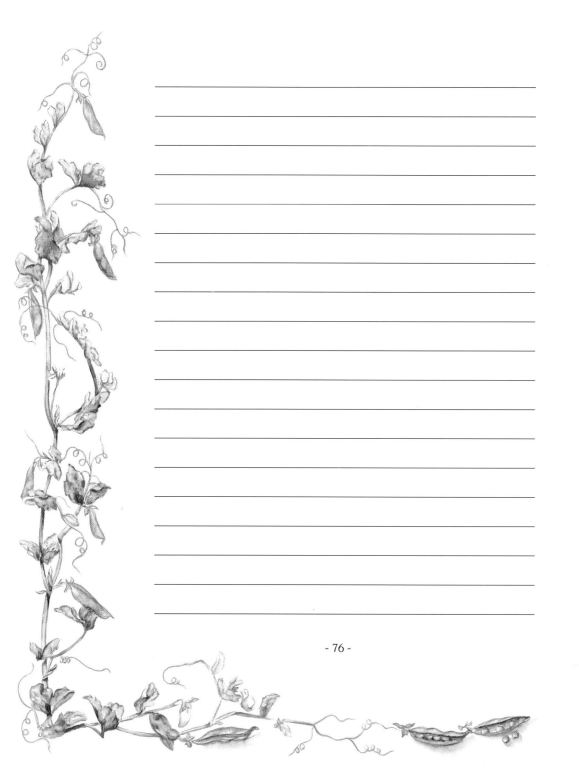

EVERYDAY PLEASURES

⌖

Traditions to Liven Up Your Days

Everyday traditions are a way of reminding ourselves what we consider important and unique in our lives. Our traditions may be whimsical, serious, or reverent by turns, depending on our family's style and sense of humor. But they are important. Recent research reinforces what families have instinctively known for centuries: traditions are good for our health and give a boost to resilience and self-esteem. So do something once, consider doing it again, and you're on your way toward starting a tradition.

Sunday-night reading: Every Sunday after dinner we would all pile onto my parents' four-poster bed and Dad would read poems and stories from favorite books in his great, deep voice. At one point he attempted to teach us about the Civil War but was met with general apathy amongst his troops. His stirring weekly rendition of Lewis Carroll's "Jabberwocky," including the booming "snicker-snack!" crescendo, was more to our taste. This was always his last act before sending us off to bed with all those nonsense words still swirling in our heads.

∽

The dollar tradition: Whenever someone in our family does something extraordinary, Dad sends them a dollar. This tradition began when we were kids and refuses to die, even though we're all grown. The day my brother-in-law turned fifty, Dad sent him a dollar. When my husband got a promotion, he called Dad to ask, "Where's my dollar?"

∽

Love notes: When my daughter was a teenager, we had difficulty communicating. So we began to leave notes for each other in hidden places to express our feelings. Sometimes I'd find a message stuck to my pillow, or she might find one from me in her sweater drawer. We survived those years with our sense of humor and love for each other intact.

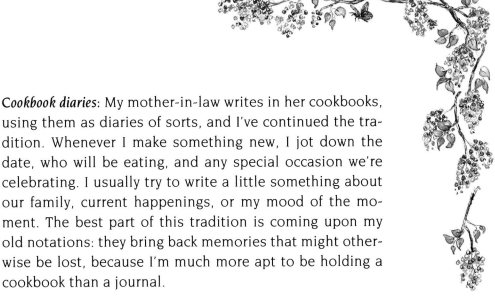

Cookbook diaries: My mother-in-law writes in her cookbooks, using them as diaries of sorts, and I've continued the tradition. Whenever I make something new, I jot down the date, who will be eating, and any special occasion we're celebrating. I usually try to write a little something about our family, current happenings, or my mood of the moment. The best part of this tradition is coming upon my old notations: they bring back memories that might otherwise be lost, because I'm much more apt to be holding a cookbook than a journal.

∽

A *mammogram and a meal*: My friends and I don't forget our annual mammograms because five of us go together for mutual strength and support. For the last four years, I've made a block of afternoon appointments for the group, one right after the other. (I call the clinic months in advance; we're juggling lots of calendars!) Next, I send out theme invitations with the date and time. (My "Return of the Twin Peaks" invitation was particularly memorable.) Our husbands join us for dinner at a nice restaurant afterward. This group event puts a pleasant spin on a stressful day.

The rubber chicken: My husband and I have a crazy way of keeping the romance going in our marriage. It's a rubber chicken. We hide it to surprise each other, and it turns up in the oddest places. Once before a trip I stuck the chicken in my husband's luggage. Another time he hid it in a bag of winter gear; I found it the following winter wearing my hat. At times, we've even forgotten where we've stashed the hapless bird. For a while we mourned our seemingly lost chicken, until it popped out of my husband's golf bag. We never know where it'll turn up next.

The semiannual meeting: Twice a year — usually on our summer vacation and around the New Year — my husband and I carve out a private hour for our semiannual meeting. First we write down our goals for the next six months, which run the gamut from individual concerns to couple goals. Then we pull out our calculators and figure out how we're faring financially. Clarifying our vision twice a year helps us achieve what we're after, and sometimes unfulfilled goals are replaced by more timely concerns.

Family huddle: Every time someone in our family is going away, we bid them farewell with our traditional family huddle. We form a circle with our arms around each other's shoulders and chant *We Love You We Love You We Love You* on and on. Call us corny but it's a winning send-off.

Garden path: In my native China, garden paths always zigzag to keep away the evil spirits, which tradition holds can only travel in a straight line. When I moved to this country I continued to build my garden walkways in this same manner to remind me of my homeland. I was pleased when I visited my son and daughter-in-law's new home, and there was their garden . . . with a zigzag path. The tradition lives on.

Moving the knobs: Many years ago, we splurged and bought beautiful blue-and-white porcelain knobs for the kitchen cabinets in our first home. When we moved, those knobs were too special to leave behind, so we unscrewed them and brought them along. Now, six houses later, they're still with us, and installing them on another set of cabinets is part of our moving-in ritual. Those knobs have practically become part of our family.

The answer is yes: My five-year-old is always asking for things, and I'm afraid I have to say no more often than I say yes. But every once in a while, when I'm fairly certain what the request will be, I use a trick learned from my own father. "The answer is YES!" I announce, even before the request is fully articulated. I remember how this response used to thrill me, and it's delightful to see my child's eyes light up as I repeat the magic words today.

Welcoming hands: In Thailand, where I grew up, instead of hugging as a form of greeting, we *wai*; that is, we put our hands together and bow our heads. We don't *wai* every friend we meet, only those older people we honor and respect. For instance, we *wai* our mother every night before bed, and when we arrive home from school each day. Even though we are Americans now, we still maintain this tradition with family and close friends.

The pink tie: It started with a pink leather tie, a gift from a law school friend who dressed in a decidedly unconventional manner. Maybe she thought I should lighten up. My new job with a law firm didn't afford much opportunity for pink leather, but when I wore the tie out in the evenings, everyone loved it. One Friday, when the partners were out of town, I wore the tie to work. I got such a positive reaction — comments, compliments, and smiles all day — that I was hooked. Now, Fridays are always wild-tie days. People count on it. It's become part of my life, a little levity I use to balance a high-pressure job.

Newspaper drop-off: My daughter and I love the spirited elderly woman next door. Every morning on our way to the school bus, we drop her newspaper on her front porch. It saves her a trip to the end of the driveway and lets her know we're thinking of her.

Seasonal get-togethers: The big kitchen in our home is perfect for cooking with friends. A winter workshop luncheon is the first of five I have each year: We make soups, and everyone brings containers for taking some home to freeze. Come spring, we share herb cuttings and slips of plants and hang flowers upside down in my garage to dry for the fall. Summer is perfect for making chutneys and canning produce from our gardens and the farmers' market. In the fall, we collect more dried flowers and leaves and make wreaths, bouquets, and centerpieces. Then, just before the holidays, our finale is a cookie-baking spree. We sample everything, and hope there's enough left over to fill our cookie tins.

ᔍ

Time with Mom: The hectic pace of our four-child household keeps me so busy with day-to-day responsibilities that I have little time left to discover what's going on with whom. So every few months I make a date to spend an afternoon or evening with each child individually. Sometimes we have pizza and see a movie, sometimes just take a quiet stroll in the park. The goal is unhurried time together so I can catch up with their lives and we can discuss what's on their minds.

_____
_____
_____
_____
_____
_____
_____
_____
_____
_____
_____
_____
_____
_____
_____
_____
_____
_____
_____

FAMILY TREES

These trees are for recording your personal family history.

CREDITS

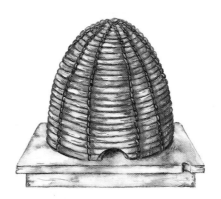